Devil Sticks for the complete Klutz

By John Cassidy & Dan Roddick

KLUTZ

Book Design: Jill Turney

Cover: William Rieser

Comic Ilustrations: Ed Taber

Instructional Ilustrations: Darwen & Vally Hennings

Photography: Peter Fox

Technical Advice & Live Reference: Seth Golub

Cover Models: Dan Gilman, John Mone & Cassie Meresman

4 1 5 8 5 7 0 8 8 8
ISBN 1-57054-088-8

WRITE US.
Klutz is an independent publisher located in Palo Alto, California and staffed entirely by real human beings. We would love to hear your comments regarding this or any of our books.

KLUTZ®
455 Portage Avenue
Palo Alto, CA 94306

ADDITIONAL COPIES
For the location of your nearest Klutz retailer, call (415) 857-0888. Should they be tragically out of stock, additional copies of this book, as well as the entire library of "100% Klutz certified" books, are available in our mail order catalogue. See back page.

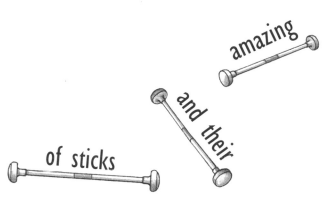

movement

amazing

and their

of sticks

The study

stickology 101

Stickology 101

This is a book about sticks, you, and gravity.

Everything is included: The sticks are in the attached bag. You are, hopefully, somewhere near at hand, and gravity we are providing free with every purchase.

The goal of the book is to enable you to juggle one stick with two other sticks you're supposed to be holding—one in each hand. If this sounds a little difficult—you're onto the whole point. It **IS** a little tricky. Or at least it looks that way.

But fortunately, that's what juggling is all about, getting tricky. And, even more fortunately, it's also about doing things that **look a little more difficult than they really are**.

4

Juggling sticks is an ancient dance, probably invent-
ed within a day or two of what we will now call
"Ordinary Juggling" (done with balls and
bare hands). But, since humans are tool
kinds of animals, juggling sticks is almost a
full notch farther up the evolutionary lad-
der. On top of that, juggling with sticks provides
an extra thrill: You not only get the sense of
tweaking gravity, you get the added thrill of **doing
it all by remote control**.

Stick juggling, done even **reasonably** well, gives
the impression that you have some sort of spe-
cial deal going with Mr. Gravity. Mr. G. is, of
course, our constant playmate in all these
endeavors and our real triumphs happen when
we can fool the eye into seeing his usual
rules suspended.

What's In the Bag?

Three **sticks**. It looks as if there are six sticks, but that's because they're taken apart so they fit in the bag.

Turn the six sticks into three sticks by screwing the pieces together.

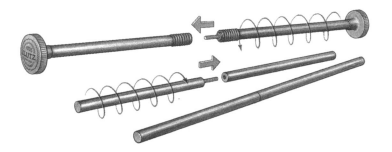

What do devil sticks have to do with the devil?

Actually, nothing. Stick play is as ancient and fundamental as ball play, and no one will ever know who the first stick player was, or where she lived. The name "devil stick" probably comes from 17th-century England, where Chinese spinning tops and stick play were recently arrived novelties from the Far East. Instead of using the unpronounceable Chinese names, the name "diabolo" was coined, perhaps from a couple of Greek words meaning "to toss across." In any event, "diabolo" was further warped into "devil" when it crossed the Atlantic to these shores.

What should I call these sticks?

The two sticks that don't have end caps on their ends go in your hands. We'll try to keep it all simple and call them **hand sticks**. The other one, with the end caps on the ends, the one that will soon be performing amazing, astonishing acrobatic feats between your hands—we'll call that one the **flip stick**.

But aren't they *really* called devil sticks?

Actually, to be painfully precise, traditional devil sticks are slightly different: The flip stick is tapered in the middle, and it doesn't have end caps. Nor, for that matter, does it have anything on it to make it less slippy. By adding a grip surface to your sticks—and caps on either end—we've made these sticks a little easier to deal with.

The Grounded
Back & Forth

You won't read
this section,
but you should.

Sit down.

Set your flip stick on the
ground in front of you.

Set it upright.

Now, leaving one of its ends on
the ground, bat it back and
forth hand to hand (*tick... tock*).
Don't do this for more than 30
seconds. It's only an icebreaker
to get you started.

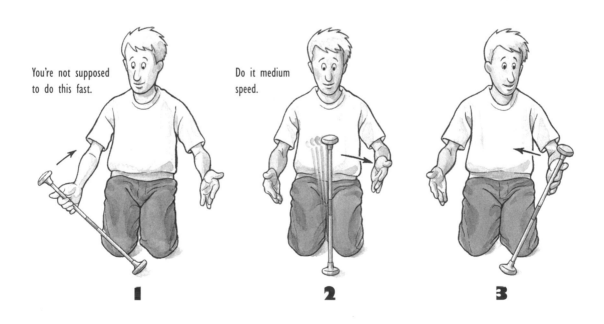

You're not supposed
to do this fast.

Do it medium
speed.

1   2   3

The Lifted
Back & Forth

An exercise not quite so boring.

Get your hands farther and farther apart so the stick falls farther and farther. Find the balance point on the stick that allows you to lift slowly **and kind of dump the flip stick over to the other hand**. If things are going well, the lower end of the stick should be lifting off the ground. Resist the urge to bring the other hand over to meet the stick. This is the last time we'll be doing anything with bare hands. From here on, you'll be using your hand sticks.

← Try to keep this end off the ground.

1

2

3

The Basic
Trapped Tick Tock
(on the ground)

Now we're going to use the hand sticks.

Still warming up but at least it's more fun.

Pick up your hand sticks, one per hand. Stay seated because you're going to be dropping a lot, and if you're sitting down, the floor is nearby.

Do a tick tock back and forth. Keep one end of the flip stick on the ground. Your hand sticks should hit the middle of each flip stick side. Keep going for a full 30 seconds. Then go on to the next page.

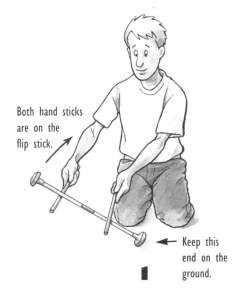

Both hand sticks are on the flip stick.

← Keep this end on the ground.

1

2

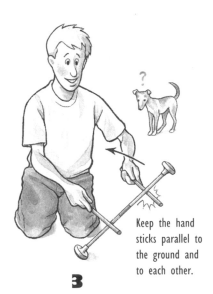

Keep the hand sticks parallel to the ground and to each other.

3

Basic Trapped Tick Tock
(off the ground)

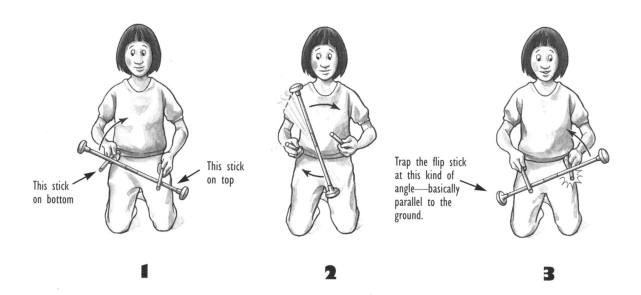

This stick on bottom

This stick on top

Trap the flip stick at this kind of angle—basically parallel to the ground.

1   **2**   **3**

The Only Rule of Devil Sticking:

DON'T bat the stick. Use your hand sticks to CATCH and TOSS. Be gentle, and be slow!

Stay on your knees.

You'll be dropping a lot on this step. But don't worry, it builds character.

This step is the same as the last warm-up except now you're lifting the flip stick off the ground.

In case you're wondering, you need two sticks because the underneath hand stick does the lifting. The other one—the trapping hand stick—just stops it from spinning too much.

Basic untrapped Tick Tock

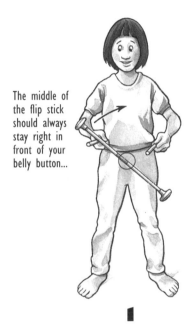

The middle of the flip stick should always stay right in front of your belly button...

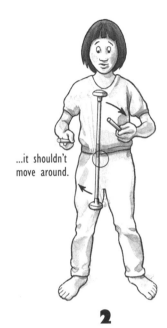

...it shouldn't move around.

Your hands move in a straight UP and DOWN line. This is a PRIME RULE of devil sticking.

1

2

3

The Only Other Rule of Devil Sticking:

Your hand sticks always move UP and DOWN. No angles. Just plain old UP and DOWN.

As you get the basic tick tock under control (and this won't happen overnight), try doing it with just one hand stick.
Don't whap it back and forth; think "catch and toss," "slow and steady."

As you get better you have our permission to stand up and later to get up on a chair and after that a big stepladder.

A Full Flip Tick Tock

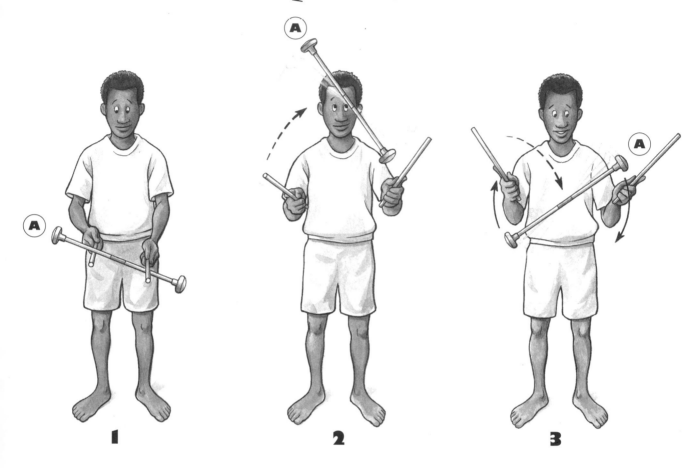

When the blessed day comes that you can do a basic two-stick tick tock standing up you will soon be looking for additional challenges to impress your friends.

Try this:
From a basic two-stick tick tock, flip it a little higher and catch it after a 360° spin. Do it with both hand sticks.

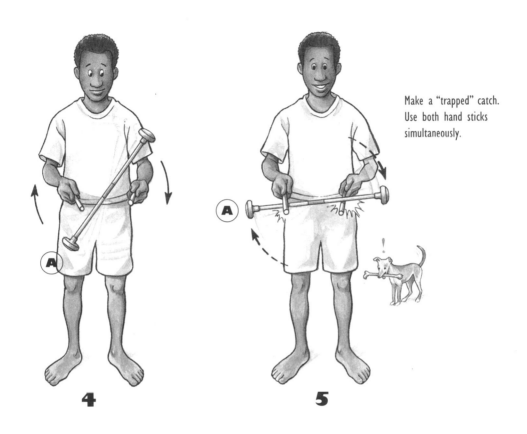

Make a "trapped" catch.
Use both hand sticks
simultaneously.

4

5

What if a full flip isn't enough of a challenge for me?

For more than a full flip, just increase the height of your toss and the speed of your spin. If you get more than 25 spins in a single toss, send us a card. We'd be impressed!

Changing Planes

Turning your flip stick into a helicopter

The flip stick will be spinning in this plane.

When you did the lifted tick tock wrong, when you let your hand sticks get screwy to each other, the flip stick started to spin like a helicopter blade. Before, this was a mistake. Now we're going to turn it into an awesome trick.

How? By going with that mistake. By pushing it so it speeds up and keeps going.

Warning: Don't try this until you can flip a tick tock with style and confidence.

Lift and "pull" a little with this right hand stick.

1

2

Your hand sticks "saw" back and forth a little to get the spin going.

3

To get a full helicopter spin, **push** and **pull** with your hand sticks while you're doing a lifted tick tock. If there were a better way to describe this trick in words, we'd use it. Unfortunately, there isn't, so look at the pictures.

This is the helicopter spin seen from over your shoulder.

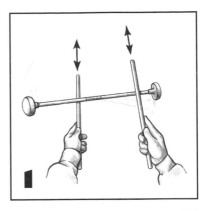

1

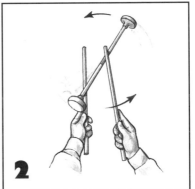

2

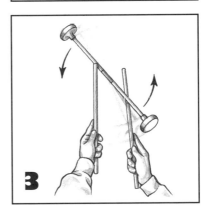

3

4

4

Pizza Toss

Don't even think about doing this trick until you can do a controlled helicopter.

Once you have your flip stick spinning in a good helicopter motion, pop it from underneath. Do it at the midpoint of the flip stick.

1

Watch it spin a few times...

2

When you get your helicopter rolling and under control (and this will take many **days**), toss it up in the air, let it spin a few times and catch it. When you toss and catch, do it from a point dead-middle on the flip stick. When you can do a good-looking pizza toss, you'll know you're a real devil sticker.

...and catch it at the midpoint.

3

4

The Propeller

An advanced one-handed trick

No move has as much sheer "How'd ya do that ?" potential as the high-speed, one-handed vertical spin. It really looks impossible, but once you get the hang of it you'll be able to count on the propeller spin as a pretty reliable part of your play.

Note for people with back problems: Practicing the propeller involves a million drops. You may want to go back to the ground like you did for your first back-and-forth exercise. It will greatly reduce your downtime.

You only need to touch the flip stick right here, to give it a lift.

Don't touch the flip stick here, just follow it around.

1

2

3

4

To get started, begin a normal tick tock series. (What's that? Look on page 10 for the pictures.)

Right in the middle of the tick tock series, pull out one of the sticks.

What will happen? The flip stick will instantly fall on your foot.

What *should* happen? You should keep the spin going with only one stick, which does a kind of stirring move. Exactly how you do this is, once again, almost impossible to state in words—look at the pictures and practice in short bursts.

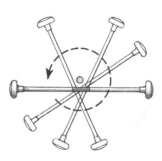

The full speed propeller spin

You will discover that in order to keep the vertical spin going you need to give a quick lift each time you go through the bottom and upward portion of the spin. You'll get it. **Just play, play, play.**

You're still not touching the flip stick until it gets to...

...here.

5

6

7

8

contortions

Twisting your body into weird shapes

There are all kinds of challenging variations to the moves you've learned so far. Adding them to your repertoire is really what makes it all hang together. For instance, all of the flips can be done under the leg or behind the back. It's just a matter of getting the move under good control and making a smooth transition to the new arm positions.

Under the Leg

Here's one way to do it...

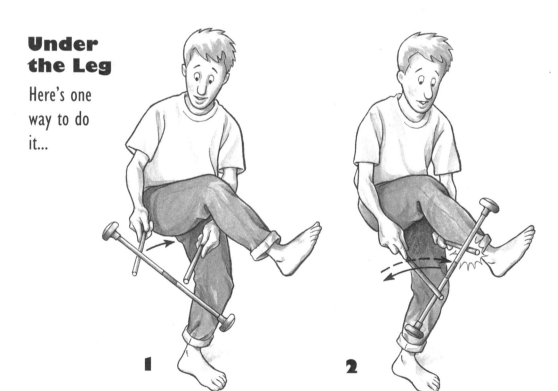

1

2

As you get these down, try going directly from one to another, linking each move to the next. If you're really limber, all kinds of contorted positions are possible. Try as many as you dare. All it takes is a lot of practice.

Speaking of practice, it's probably best not to even think of what you're doing as practice. Lawyers practice. Football players call 4 hours in the heat of August practice. We're really just playing here, aren't we? The big difference is that you can stop whenever you aren't having fun. Folks who study how we learn things assure us that we learn much more easily when we're really into it. Take this trip in short, pleasant jaunts, not a death march. You don't want to get there too quickly anyway. The fun is in the going.

...Here's another.

1

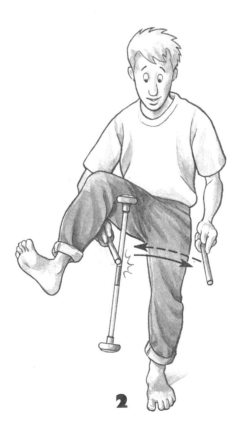

2

Even More Contortions

When you can do a basic tick tock between your legs, with crossed arms, or behind the back you know you're into the advanced stages of *fulminating devil stickitis*. Although it's not shown here, you can do variations on all of these that make them even more difficult. Consult your chiropractor.

Between Both Legs

If you're short, this is tough. Try getting up on your toes.

Crossed Arms

The idea is to leave your arms crossed as you tick tock back and forth. Not easy!

In the rare event of a drop

The condition of your back will probably determine whether or not you'll want to bend down each time to recover the escaped stick. Use those hand sticks to make the job easier. You can probably slip the tip of one under the fallen stick and flip it up in one clean motion. Barefoot? Use your toes. Either way, do it well, and the easily amused will think it's part of the show.

Behind the Back

Your ultimate goal: normal tick tock. Quick switch to crossed arms. Quick switch to behind the back. Quick switch back to normal. Incredible.

Miscellaneous Tricks

What follows is a select grab bag of additional challenge. If you're this far into the book, you should already be over the first frustrating stages of tick tocking, so dropping sticks and bending over to pick them up should be second nature to you by now. (Which is good, since you'll be doing a lot of it as you get into these more advanced kinds of things.)

But there's also a relentless momentum that gets going right around here, too. If you can do even one of these tricks, you are treading dangerously close to full-bore stick competence, and that is something that feeds on itself with each new trick.

At some point in here, if you glance down, you will find your feet already tripping down the shining path to Total Cosmic Stick Meister. It's a long road, with absolutely no last and final destination, but it's a fun trip all the way.

Arm Rollover

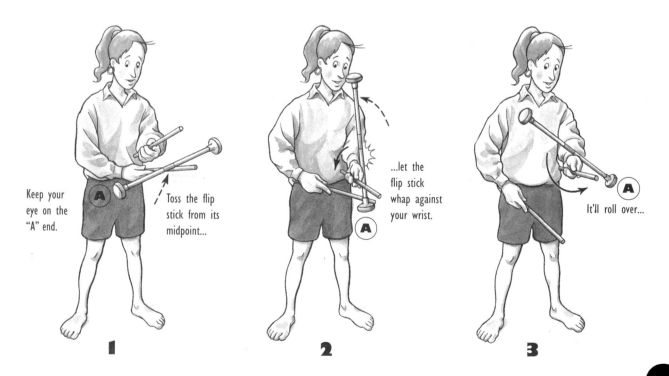

Keep your eye on the "A" end.

Toss the flip stick from its midpoint...

...let the flip stick whap against your wrist.

It'll roll over...

1   **2**   **3**

Leg Rollover

Toss the flip stick from its midpoint.

1

Let it roll over your leg...

...and catch.

2

...like this.

Ⓐ

4

Catch it back on...

Ⓐ

5

...the midpoint.

Ⓐ

6

Stick Rollover

(This trick is almost identical to the Arm Rollover.)

Watch the "A" end.

Toss the flip stick from its midpoint.

The flip stick hits the hand stick...

...and rolls...

1

2

3

One Stick Tick Tock

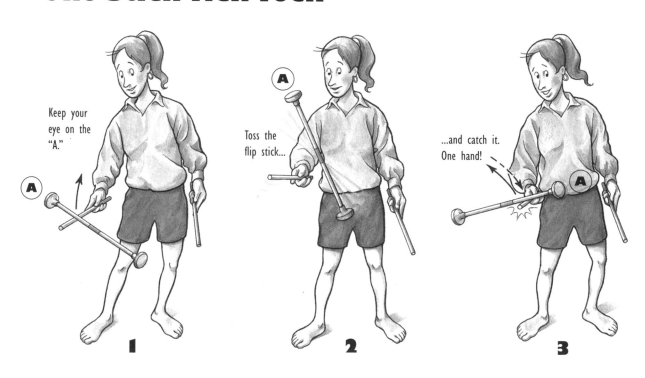

Keep your eye on the "A."

Toss the flip stick...

...and catch it. One hand!

1

2

3

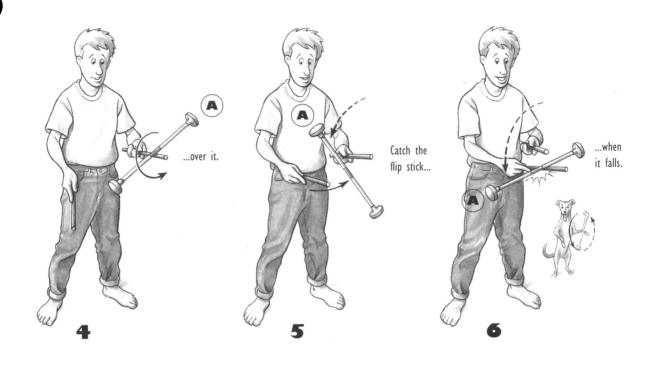

4 ...over it.

5 Catch the flip stick...

6 ...when it falls.

Buzz Saw

Spin the flip stick as shown. (Count on a lot of drops.)

Master these tricks and amaze your friends!

No Touch Hopover

Toss the flip stick <u>over</u> the hand stick.

Watch the "A" end.

A

The flip stick never touches this hand stick.

A

A

The hand stick never moves. It's the hurdle.

1

2

3

Wrist Rollover

Catch the flip stick between the underside of your wrist and the end of the hand stick.

A

A

Rotate your wrist clockwise so the flip stick rolls around it.

A

A

A

1

2

3

Don't forget!
The flip stick
should clear
this hand stick.
No touching!

Lonely?

Try tandem tricks.

Passing

If you have a friend (or three) who can manage a basic tick tock and who have their own hand sticks, try tossing the flip stick back and forth. This can be done at a fast and furious pace once all the players get some experience.

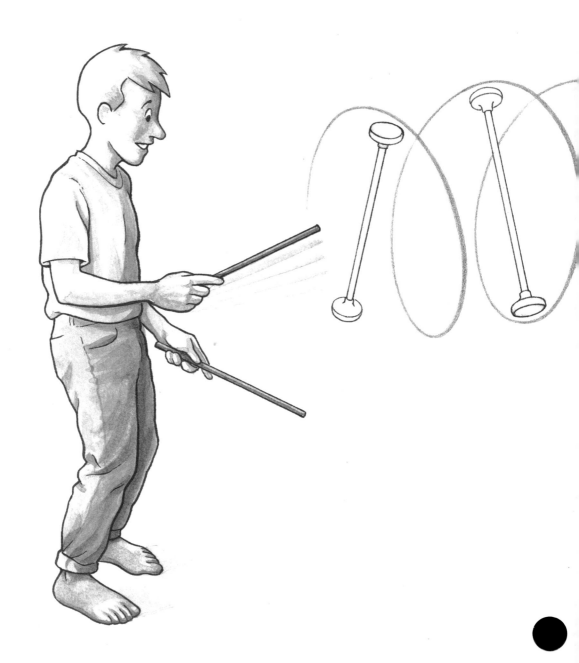

Freestyle Challenge

Once you've got a trick you'd like to show off, and a friend or two similarly inspired, play a game of Challenge. The rules are simple: Go through your trick or routine and toss the flip stick over to your partner who then has to duplicate it. If he or she can't, that's a "D" for them. Two drops means "DE"...three drops, "DEV"...and so forth to "DEVIL."

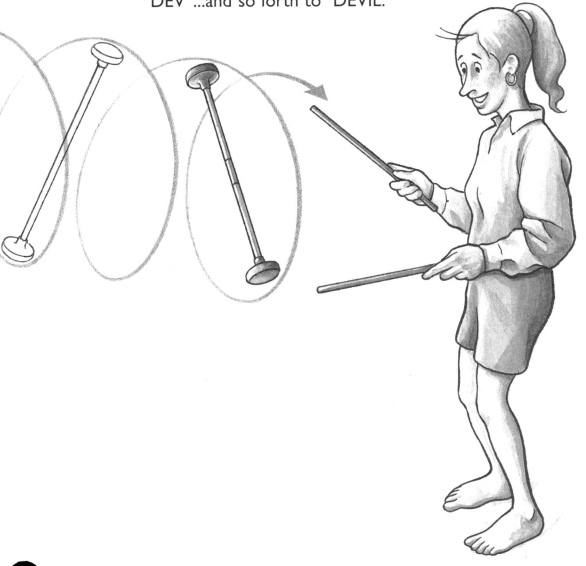

31

More TaNDem

A lot of the tricks in this book can be done by two people with only one set of hand sticks (in other words, one hand stick per player). Both players have to be at least fairly competent before this will work. Start with the basic tick tock and test yourselves. If you're still getting along after that, go forth to things more complicated. Good luck to your relationship.

Side to Side

1

2

3

Double Devil Stick Tandem Switch

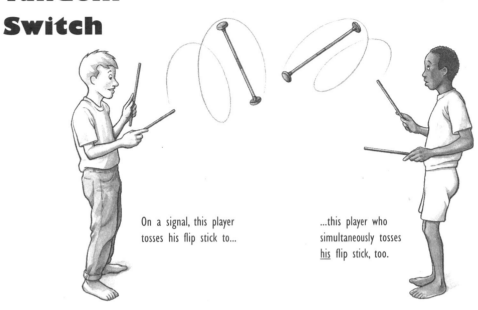

On a signal, this player tosses his flip stick to...

...this player who simultaneously tosses <u>his</u> flip stick, too.

Back to Back

1...2...3...

1

2

3

Other Books Available from
KLUTZ®

Juggling for the Complete Klutz
The Aerobie Book
The Unbelievable Bubble Book
The Foxtail Book
The Hacky Sack Book
The Official Koosh Book
Table Top Football

FREE CATALOGUE!

Filled with the entire library of "100% Klutz Certified" books, as well as a diverse collection of other things we happen to like, The Klutz Catalogue is, in all modesty, unlike any other catalogue. If you enjoyed the **Devil Sticks for the Complete Klutz** book and are interested in doing some more juggling, check out **Juggling for the Complete Klutz** by the editors of Klutz Press. For our Free Catalogue, just answer this lengthy questionnaire. Grab the nearest pen, fill in the blanks, throw on some postage, and send it our way.

Cut this part out to send to us.

Who Are You? (You wonderful person you.)

❏ Kid   ❏ Grown-up   ❏ Somewhere in-between

❏ Girl   ❏ Boy

Name _____

Address _____

City _____ State _____ Zip_____

Phone # (_____) _____

How did you first hear about the Devil Sticks book?

_____

_____

Devilstick Book

Fold along this line.

True or False?

T   F
❏   ❏   Someone gave me this book as a gift because they like me a whole lot!

❏   ❏   I bought this book for myself because I deserve it!

❏   ❏   This is the first **KLUTZ** book I've ever bought.

A Personal Question!

I'm the kind of person who spends this kind of money on a gift for a friend:

❏ Less than $10   ❏ $10–$15   ❏ $15–$20   ❏ $20–$25

❏ For the right gift, whatever it's worth!

My Bright Ideas!

What would you like us to write a book about?

_____

Complaints here. ❏ (Please don't go outside the box)

KLUTZ®

Catalogue
455 Portage Avenue
Palo Alto, CA 94306

You can staple this
postcard closed here